40 Skewer Recipes for Home

By: Kelly Johnson

Table of Contents

Chicken Skewers:
- Grilled Lemon Garlic Chicken Skewers
- Teriyaki Chicken Skewers
- Honey Mustard Chicken Skewers
- Coconut Lime Chicken Skewers
- Tandoori Chicken Skewers
- BBQ Ranch Chicken Skewers
- Spicy Sriracha Chicken Skewers
- Maple Dijon Glazed Chicken Skewers
- Pesto Chicken Caprese Skewers
- Mediterranean Chicken Souvlaki Skewers

Beef Skewers:
- Garlic Herb Steak Skewers
- Korean BBQ Beef Skewers
- Balsamic Rosemary Beef Skewers
- Moroccan Spiced Beef Skewers
- Cajun Blackened Beef Skewers
- Thai Basil Beef Skewers
- Chimichurri Marinated Beef Skewers
- Sesame Ginger Beef Skewers
- Honey Soy Glazed Beef Skewers
- Blue Cheese-Stuffed Bacon Wrapped Beef Skew

Seafood Skewers:
- Lemon Herb Shrimp Skewers
- Cajun Spiced Salmon Skewers
- Coconut Lime Grilled Scallop Skewers
- Teriyaki Glazed Tuna Skewers
- Mediterranean Grilled Swordfish Skewers
- Garlic Butter Lobster Skewers
- Pineapple Glazed Mahi-Mahi Skewers
- Cilantro Lime Grilled Snapper Skewers
- Spicy Mango Salsa Shrimp Skewers
- Chipotle Lime Grilled Prawn Skewers

Vegetarian Skewers:
- Caprese Salad Skewers
- Balsamic Glazed Veggie Skewers
- Grilled Halloumi and Vegetable Skewers
- Teriyaki Tofu Skewers
- Greek Salad Skewers with Feta
- Indian Spiced Paneer Skewers
- Pesto Zucchini and Tomato Skewers
- Harissa Roasted Vegetable Skewers
- Stuffed Mushroom Skewers
- Sweet and Spicy Pineapple Jalapeño Skewers

Chicken Skewers:

Grilled Lemon Garlic Chicken Skewers

Ingredients:

- 1.5 lbs boneless, skinless chicken breasts, cut into bite-sized cubes
- 3 tablespoons olive oil
- 3 cloves garlic, minced
- 2 tablespoons fresh lemon juice
- 1 teaspoon lemon zest
- 1 teaspoon dried oregano
- 1 teaspoon dried thyme
- Salt and black pepper to taste
- Wooden skewers, soaked in water for 30 minutes

Instructions:

In a bowl, combine olive oil, minced garlic, lemon juice, lemon zest, dried oregano, dried thyme, salt, and black pepper. Mix well to create the marinade.

Place the chicken cubes in a resealable plastic bag or shallow dish. Pour the marinade over the chicken, ensuring all pieces are well-coated. Seal the bag or cover the dish and refrigerate for at least 2 hours, allowing the flavors to meld.

Preheat your grill to medium-high heat.

Thread the marinated chicken cubes onto the soaked wooden skewers, distributing them evenly.

Grill the skewers for about 8-10 minutes, turning occasionally, until the chicken is fully cooked and has a nice char.

Optionally, brush some extra marinade on the skewers during grilling for added flavor.

Once done, remove the skewers from the grill and let them rest for a few minutes.

Serve the grilled lemon garlic chicken skewers with your favorite dipping sauce or a side of rice and vegetables.

Enjoy these succulent and flavorful grilled lemon garlic chicken skewers!

Teriyaki Chicken Skewers

Ingredients:

- 1.5 lbs boneless, skinless chicken thighs, cut into bite-sized pieces
- 1/2 cup soy sauce
- 1/4 cup mirin
- 2 tablespoons sake (or dry white wine)
- 2 tablespoons brown sugar
- 2 cloves garlic, minced
- 1 teaspoon fresh ginger, grated
- 1 tablespoon sesame oil
- 1 tablespoon cornstarch (optional, for thickening)
- Wooden skewers, soaked in water for 30 minutes

Instructions:

In a bowl, whisk together soy sauce, mirin, sake, brown sugar, minced garlic, grated ginger, and sesame oil to create the teriyaki marinade.

Place the chicken pieces in a resealable plastic bag or shallow dish. Pour half of the teriyaki marinade over the chicken, reserving the other half for basting and serving. Seal the bag or cover the dish and marinate in the refrigerator for at least 1-2 hours.

Preheat your grill to medium-high heat.

Thread the marinated chicken pieces onto the soaked wooden skewers.

Grill the skewers for approximately 8-10 minutes, turning and basting with the reserved teriyaki sauce occasionally, until the chicken is fully cooked and caramelized.

If you prefer a thicker sauce, mix the cornstarch with a tablespoon of water, add it to the remaining teriyaki sauce, and simmer on the stove until thickened.

Once done, remove the skewers from the grill and let them rest for a few minutes. Serve the teriyaki chicken skewers over a bed of steamed rice or with your favorite stir-fried vegetables. Drizzle the thickened teriyaki sauce over the top for extra flavor.

Enjoy these delicious Teriyaki Chicken Skewers with the perfect balance of sweet and savory flavors!

Honey Mustard Chicken Skewers

Ingredients:

- 1.5 lbs boneless, skinless chicken breasts, cut into cubes
- 1/4 cup Dijon mustard
- 1/4 cup honey
- 2 tablespoons whole grain mustard
- 2 tablespoons olive oil
- 2 cloves garlic, minced
- 1 teaspoon dried thyme
- Salt and black pepper to taste
- Wooden skewers, soaked in water for 30 minutes

Instructions:

In a bowl, whisk together Dijon mustard, honey, whole grain mustard, olive oil, minced garlic, dried thyme, salt, and black pepper to create the honey mustard marinade.

Place the chicken cubes in a resealable plastic bag or shallow dish. Pour the honey mustard marinade over the chicken, ensuring all pieces are well-coated. Seal the bag or cover the dish and refrigerate for at least 1-2 hours.

Preheat your grill to medium-high heat.

Thread the marinated chicken cubes onto the soaked wooden skewers, distributing them evenly.

Grill the skewers for about 8-10 minutes, turning occasionally, until the chicken is fully cooked and has a golden brown exterior.

Optionally, brush some extra marinade on the skewers during grilling for added flavor.

Once done, remove the skewers from the grill and let them rest for a few minutes.

Serve the honey mustard chicken skewers with a side of rice, quinoa, or a fresh salad.

Enjoy these sweet and tangy Honey Mustard Chicken Skewers for a delightful meal!

Coconut Lime Chicken Skewers

Ingredients:

- 1.5 lbs boneless, skinless chicken thighs, cut into bite-sized pieces
- 1 cup coconut milk
- Zest and juice of 2 limes
- 3 tablespoons soy sauce
- 2 tablespoons fish sauce
- 2 tablespoons brown sugar
- 2 cloves garlic, minced
- 1 tablespoon fresh ginger, grated
- 1 teaspoon ground coriander
- Wooden skewers, soaked in water for 30 minutes

Instructions:

In a bowl, combine coconut milk, lime zest, lime juice, soy sauce, fish sauce, brown sugar, minced garlic, grated ginger, and ground coriander to create the marinade.

Place the chicken pieces in a resealable plastic bag or shallow dish. Pour the coconut lime marinade over the chicken, ensuring all pieces are well-coated. Seal the bag or cover the dish and refrigerate for at least 2 hours.

Preheat your grill to medium-high heat.

Thread the marinated chicken pieces onto the soaked wooden skewers.

Grill the skewers for approximately 8-10 minutes, turning occasionally, until the chicken is fully cooked and has a light char.

While grilling, you can brush some additional marinade on the skewers for extra flavor.

Once done, remove the skewers from the grill and let them rest for a few minutes. Serve the coconut lime chicken skewers with a side of coconut rice and a sprinkle of fresh cilantro.

Enjoy these Coconut Lime Chicken Skewers with a tropical and zesty flavor profile!

Tandoori Chicken Skewers

Ingredients:

For the Marinade:

- 1.5 lbs boneless, skinless chicken thighs, cut into bite-sized pieces
- 1 cup plain yogurt
- 3 tablespoons Tandoori spice blend
- 2 tablespoons ginger paste
- 2 tablespoons garlic paste
- 1 tablespoon ground coriander
- 1 tablespoon ground cumin
- 1 teaspoon turmeric powder
- 1 teaspoon cayenne pepper (adjust to taste)
- 2 tablespoons lemon juice
- Salt to taste
- Wooden skewers, soaked in water for 30 minutes

For Garnish:

- Fresh cilantro, chopped
- Lemon wedges

Instructions:

In a large bowl, combine yogurt, Tandoori spice blend, ginger paste, garlic paste, ground coriander, ground cumin, turmeric powder, cayenne pepper, lemon juice, and salt. Mix well to create the marinade.

Add the chicken pieces to the marinade, making sure each piece is thoroughly coated. Cover the bowl and marinate in the refrigerator for at least 4 hours or preferably overnight.

Preheat your grill to medium-high heat.

Thread the marinated chicken pieces onto the soaked wooden skewers.

Grill the skewers for approximately 10-12 minutes, turning occasionally, until the chicken is fully cooked and has a beautiful char from the Tandoori spices.

Once done, remove the skewers from the grill and let them rest for a few minutes. Garnish the Tandoori chicken skewers with fresh chopped cilantro and serve with lemon wedges on the side.

Enjoy these Tandoori Chicken Skewers with naan bread, rice, or a cooling cucumber yogurt sauce.

Savor the authentic flavors of Tandoori cuisine with these delicious chicken skewers!

BBQ Ranch Chicken Skewers

Ingredients:

For the Marinade:

- 1.5 lbs boneless, skinless chicken breasts, cut into cubes
- 1/2 cup BBQ sauce
- 1/4 cup ranch dressing
- 2 tablespoons olive oil
- 2 tablespoons honey
- 1 teaspoon smoked paprika
- 1 teaspoon onion powder
- 1 teaspoon garlic powder
- Salt and black pepper to taste
- Wooden skewers, soaked in water for 30 minutes

For Basting and Serving:

- Additional BBQ sauce
- Additional ranch dressing
- Fresh parsley, chopped (for garnish)

Instructions:

In a bowl, whisk together BBQ sauce, ranch dressing, olive oil, honey, smoked paprika, onion powder, garlic powder, salt, and black pepper to create the marinade.

Place the chicken cubes in a resealable plastic bag or shallow dish. Pour the BBQ ranch marinade over the chicken, ensuring all pieces are well-coated. Seal the bag or cover the dish and refrigerate for at least 2 hours.

Preheat your grill to medium-high heat.

Thread the marinated chicken cubes onto the soaked wooden skewers.

Grill the skewers for about 8-10 minutes, turning occasionally, until the chicken is fully cooked and has a nice caramelized exterior.

During grilling, baste the skewers with additional BBQ sauce for added flavor.

Once done, remove the skewers from the grill and let them rest for a few minutes.

Serve the BBQ Ranch Chicken Skewers with a side of ranch dressing for dipping, and garnish with fresh chopped parsley.

Enjoy these savory and tangy BBQ Ranch Chicken Skewers for a delightful barbecue experience!

Spicy Sriracha Chicken Skewers

Ingredients:

For the Marinade:

- 1.5 lbs boneless, skinless chicken thighs, cut into bite-sized pieces
- 1/4 cup soy sauce
- 3 tablespoons Sriracha sauce
- 2 tablespoons honey
- 2 tablespoons rice vinegar
- 2 tablespoons sesame oil
- 2 cloves garlic, minced
- 1 teaspoon ginger, grated
- 1 tablespoon sesame seeds (optional)
- Wooden skewers, soaked in water for 30 minutes

For Garnish:

- Green onions, sliced
- Lime wedges

Instructions:

In a bowl, combine soy sauce, Sriracha sauce, honey, rice vinegar, sesame oil, minced garlic, grated ginger, and sesame seeds. Mix well to create the spicy Sriracha marinade.

Place the chicken pieces in a resealable plastic bag or shallow dish. Pour the Sriracha marinade over the chicken, ensuring all pieces are well-coated. Seal the bag or cover the dish and refrigerate for at least 1-2 hours.

Preheat your grill to medium-high heat.

Thread the marinated chicken pieces onto the soaked wooden skewers.

Grill the skewers for approximately 8-10 minutes, turning occasionally, until the chicken is fully cooked and has a nice char.

Once done, remove the skewers from the grill and let them rest for a few minutes.

Garnish the Spicy Sriracha Chicken Skewers with sliced green onions and serve with lime wedges on the side.

Enjoy these fiery and flavorful Spicy Sriracha Chicken Skewers as an appetizer or main course!

Feel free to adjust the Sriracha quantity based on your spice preference.

Maple Dijon Glazed Chicken Skewers

Ingredients:

For the Marinade:

- 1.5 lbs boneless, skinless chicken breasts, cut into cubes
- 1/4 cup Dijon mustard
- 3 tablespoons maple syrup
- 2 tablespoons olive oil
- 2 cloves garlic, minced
- 1 teaspoon dried thyme
- Salt and black pepper to taste
- Wooden skewers, soaked in water for 30 minutes

For Basting and Serving:

- Additional maple syrup
- Fresh parsley, chopped (for garnish)

Instructions:

In a bowl, whisk together Dijon mustard, maple syrup, olive oil, minced garlic, dried thyme, salt, and black pepper to create the marinade.

Place the chicken cubes in a resealable plastic bag or shallow dish. Pour the Maple Dijon marinade over the chicken, ensuring all pieces are well-coated. Seal the bag or cover the dish and refrigerate for at least 1-2 hours.

Preheat your grill to medium-high heat.

Thread the marinated chicken cubes onto the soaked wooden skewers.

Grill the skewers for about 8-10 minutes, turning occasionally, until the chicken is fully cooked and has a glossy glaze.

During grilling, baste the skewers with additional maple syrup for added sweetness.

Once done, remove the skewers from the grill and let them rest for a few minutes. Serve the Maple Dijon Glazed Chicken Skewers with a drizzle of extra maple syrup and a sprinkle of fresh chopped parsley.

Enjoy these sweet and savory Maple Dijon Glazed Chicken Skewers as a delicious and elegant dish!

Pesto Chicken Caprese Skewers

Ingredients:

For the Pesto Marinade:

- 1.5 lbs boneless, skinless chicken breasts, cut into cubes
- 1 cup fresh basil leaves, packed
- 1/2 cup pine nuts
- 1/2 cup grated Parmesan cheese
- 2 cloves garlic, minced
- 1/2 cup extra-virgin olive oil
- Salt and black pepper to taste

Additional Skewer Ingredients:

- Cherry tomatoes
- Fresh mozzarella balls
- Balsamic glaze (for drizzling)
- Wooden skewers, soaked in water for 30 minutes

Instructions:

For the Pesto Marinade:

In a food processor, combine fresh basil, pine nuts, grated Parmesan cheese, and minced garlic. Pulse until coarsely chopped.
With the food processor running, slowly pour in the olive oil until the mixture becomes a smooth pesto sauce. Season with salt and black pepper to taste. Set aside.

For Assembling the Skewers:

Place the chicken cubes in a bowl and add half of the prepared pesto sauce.
Toss to coat the chicken evenly. Reserve the remaining pesto for serving.
Thread the marinated chicken cubes, cherry tomatoes, and fresh mozzarella balls onto the soaked wooden skewers, alternating between the ingredients.
Preheat your grill to medium-high heat.
Grill the skewers for about 8-10 minutes, turning occasionally, until the chicken is fully cooked and has a nice char.
Once done, remove the skewers from the grill and let them rest for a few minutes.

Drizzle the Pesto Chicken Caprese Skewers with the remaining pesto sauce and balsamic glaze before serving.
Serve these delightful skewers as a flavorful appetizer or main course.

Enjoy these Pesto Chicken Caprese Skewers for a burst of fresh and vibrant flavors!

Mediterranean Chicken Souvlaki Skewers

Ingredients:

For the Marinade:

- 1.5 lbs boneless, skinless chicken thighs, cut into bite-sized pieces
- 1/4 cup olive oil
- 2 tablespoons red wine vinegar
- 2 tablespoons lemon juice
- 2 cloves garlic, minced
- 1 teaspoon dried oregano
- 1 teaspoon dried thyme
- 1 teaspoon paprika
- Salt and black pepper to taste

Additional Skewer Ingredients:

- Cherry tomatoes
- Red onion, cut into chunks
- Tzatziki sauce (for serving)
- Wooden skewers, soaked in water for 30 minutes

Instructions:

For the Marinade:

In a bowl, whisk together olive oil, red wine vinegar, lemon juice, minced garlic, dried oregano, dried thyme, paprika, salt, and black pepper to create the marinade.

Place the chicken pieces in a resealable plastic bag or shallow dish. Pour the Mediterranean marinade over the chicken, ensuring all pieces are well-coated. Seal the bag or cover the dish and refrigerate for at least 2 hours.

For Assembling the Skewers:

Preheat your grill to medium-high heat.

Thread the marinated chicken pieces, cherry tomatoes, and red onion chunks onto the soaked wooden skewers, alternating between the ingredients.

Grill the skewers for approximately 8-10 minutes, turning occasionally, until the chicken is fully cooked and has a nice char.
Once done, remove the skewers from the grill and let them rest for a few minutes.
Serve the Mediterranean Chicken Souvlaki Skewers with a side of tzatziki sauce for dipping.
Optionally, serve over a bed of rice or with warm pita bread for a complete meal.

Enjoy these flavorful Mediterranean Chicken Souvlaki Skewers for a taste of the Greek cuisine!

Beef Skewers:
Garlic Herb Steak Skewers

Ingredients:

For the Marinade:

- 1.5 lbs sirloin or flank steak, cut into bite-sized cubes
- 1/4 cup olive oil
- 4 cloves garlic, minced
- 2 tablespoons fresh parsley, chopped
- 1 tablespoon fresh rosemary, chopped
- 1 tablespoon fresh thyme, chopped
- 1 teaspoon dried oregano
- 1 teaspoon Dijon mustard
- Salt and black pepper to taste

Additional Skewer Ingredients:

- Red bell peppers, cut into chunks
- Red onion, cut into chunks
- Wooden skewers, soaked in water for 30 minutes

Instructions:

For the Marinade:

In a bowl, whisk together olive oil, minced garlic, chopped parsley, rosemary, thyme, dried oregano, Dijon mustard, salt, and black pepper to create the herb-infused marinade.

Place the beef cubes in a resealable plastic bag or shallow dish. Pour the marinade over the beef, ensuring all pieces are well-coated. Seal the bag or cover the dish and refrigerate for at least 2 hours or overnight for maximum flavor.

For Assembling the Skewers:

Preheat your grill to medium-high heat.

Thread the marinated beef cubes, red bell pepper chunks, and red onion chunks onto the soaked wooden skewers, alternating between the ingredients.

Grill the skewers for about 8-10 minutes, turning occasionally, until the beef reaches your desired level of doneness and has a nice sear.

Once done, remove the skewers from the grill and let them rest for a few minutes.
Serve the Garlic Herb Steak Skewers over a bed of quinoa or with your favorite side salad.
Garnish with additional fresh herbs for a burst of flavor.

Enjoy these succulent and aromatic Garlic Herb Steak Skewers for a delightful beef dish!

Korean BBQ Beef Skewers

Ingredients:

For the Marinade:

- 1.5 lbs beef sirloin or ribeye, thinly sliced
- 1/4 cup soy sauce
- 2 tablespoons mirin
- 2 tablespoons brown sugar
- 2 tablespoons sesame oil
- 3 cloves garlic, minced
- 1 tablespoon fresh ginger, grated
- 1 tablespoon rice vinegar
- 1 teaspoon red pepper flakes (adjust to taste)
- 2 green onions, finely chopped
- Wooden skewers, soaked in water for 30 minutes

Additional Skewer Ingredients:

- Red and green bell peppers, cut into chunks
- Pineapple chunks
- Sesame seeds (for garnish)
- Green onions, sliced (for garnish)

Instructions:

For the Marinade:

In a bowl, whisk together soy sauce, mirin, brown sugar, sesame oil, minced garlic, grated ginger, rice vinegar, red pepper flakes, and chopped green onions to create the Korean BBQ marinade.
Place the thinly sliced beef in a resealable plastic bag or shallow dish. Pour the marinade over the beef, ensuring all slices are well-coated. Seal the bag or cover the dish and refrigerate for at least 2 hours or overnight for optimal flavor.

For Assembling the Skewers:

Preheat your grill to medium-high heat.
Thread the marinated beef slices, bell pepper chunks, and pineapple chunks onto the soaked wooden skewers, alternating between the ingredients.

Grill the skewers for approximately 2-3 minutes per side, or until the beef is cooked to your liking and has a delicious caramelized exterior.
Once done, remove the skewers from the grill and let them rest for a few minutes.
Sprinkle sesame seeds and sliced green onions on top for garnish.
Serve the Korean BBQ Beef Skewers over steamed rice or with a side of kimchi for an authentic experience.

Enjoy these flavorful Korean BBQ Beef Skewers with a perfect balance of sweet, savory, and spicy notes!

Balsamic Rosemary Beef Skewers

Ingredients:

For the Marinade:

- 1.5 lbs beef sirloin or tenderloin, cut into bite-sized cubes
- 1/3 cup balsamic vinegar
- 1/4 cup olive oil
- 2 tablespoons fresh rosemary, finely chopped
- 3 cloves garlic, minced
- 1 tablespoon Dijon mustard
- 1 tablespoon honey
- Salt and black pepper to taste
- Wooden skewers, soaked in water for 30 minutes

Additional Skewer Ingredients:

- Cherry tomatoes
- Button mushrooms, cleaned and stems removed
- Red onion, cut into chunks
- Balsamic glaze (for drizzling)

Instructions:

For the Marinade:

In a bowl, whisk together balsamic vinegar, olive oil, chopped rosemary, minced garlic, Dijon mustard, honey, salt, and black pepper to create the flavorful marinade.
Place the beef cubes in a resealable plastic bag or shallow dish. Pour the balsamic rosemary marinade over the beef, ensuring all pieces are well-coated. Seal the bag or cover the dish and refrigerate for at least 2 hours.

For Assembling the Skewers:

Preheat your grill to medium-high heat.
Thread the marinated beef cubes, cherry tomatoes, mushrooms, and red onion chunks onto the soaked wooden skewers, alternating between the ingredients.

Grill the skewers for about 8-10 minutes, turning occasionally, until the beef is cooked to your liking and has a nice sear.
Once done, remove the skewers from the grill and let them rest for a few minutes.
Drizzle the Balsamic Rosemary Beef Skewers with additional balsamic glaze for extra richness.
Serve over a bed of couscous or with a side of roasted vegetables.

Enjoy these elegant and savory Balsamic Rosemary Beef Skewers as a delightful main course!

Moroccan Spiced Beef Skewers

Ingredients:

For the Marinade:

- 1.5 lbs beef sirloin or flank steak, cut into cubes
- 2 tablespoons olive oil
- 2 tablespoons ground cumin
- 1 tablespoon ground coriander
- 1 teaspoon ground cinnamon
- 1 teaspoon paprika
- 1 teaspoon ground turmeric
- 1 teaspoon ground ginger
- 3 cloves garlic, minced
- Zest and juice of 1 lemon
- Salt and black pepper to taste
- Wooden skewers, soaked in water for 30 minutes

Additional Skewer Ingredients:

- Red and yellow bell peppers, cut into chunks
- Red onion, cut into chunks
- Fresh mint leaves (for garnish)

Instructions:

For the Marinade:

In a bowl, combine olive oil, ground cumin, ground coriander, ground cinnamon, paprika, ground turmeric, ground ginger, minced garlic, lemon zest, lemon juice, salt, and black pepper to create the Moroccan spice marinade.

Place the beef cubes in a resealable plastic bag or shallow dish. Pour the Moroccan spice marinade over the beef, ensuring all pieces are well-coated. Seal the bag or cover the dish and refrigerate for at least 2 hours.

For Assembling the Skewers:

Preheat your grill to medium-high heat.

Thread the marinated beef cubes, bell pepper chunks, and red onion chunks onto the soaked wooden skewers, alternating between the ingredients.

Grill the skewers for about 8-10 minutes, turning occasionally, until the beef is cooked to your liking and has a nice char.

Once done, remove the skewers from the grill and let them rest for a few minutes.

Garnish the Moroccan Spiced Beef Skewers with fresh mint leaves.

Serve over couscous or with a side of harissa sauce for an extra kick.

Enjoy these flavorful and aromatic Moroccan Spiced Beef Skewers for a taste of North African cuisine!

Cajun Blackened Beef Skewers

Ingredients:

For the Cajun Blackening Spice Rub:

- 1.5 lbs beef sirloin or ribeye, cut into cubes
- 2 tablespoons paprika
- 1 tablespoon onion powder
- 1 tablespoon garlic powder
- 1 tablespoon dried thyme
- 1 teaspoon dried oregano
- 1 teaspoon cayenne pepper (adjust to taste)
- 1 teaspoon smoked paprika
- Salt and black pepper to taste
- Olive oil (for brushing)
- Wooden skewers, soaked in water for 30 minutes

Additional Skewer Ingredients:

- Red and green bell peppers, cut into chunks
- Red onion, cut into chunks
- Lemon wedges (for serving)

Instructions:

For the Cajun Blackening Spice Rub:

> In a bowl, mix together paprika, onion powder, garlic powder, dried thyme, dried oregano, cayenne pepper, smoked paprika, salt, and black pepper to create the Cajun blackening spice rub.
> Coat the beef cubes evenly with the Cajun spice rub, pressing the spices onto the meat.

For Assembling the Skewers:

> Preheat your grill to medium-high heat.
> Thread the Cajun blackened beef cubes, bell pepper chunks, and red onion chunks onto the soaked wooden skewers, alternating between the ingredients.
> Brush the skewers with olive oil to help with the blackening process.

Grill the skewers for about 8-10 minutes, turning occasionally, until the beef is cooked to your liking and has a flavorful blackened crust.
Once done, remove the skewers from the grill and let them rest for a few minutes.
Serve the Cajun Blackened Beef Skewers with lemon wedges on the side.

Enjoy these boldly seasoned Cajun Blackened Beef Skewers for a spicy and savory delight!

Thai Basil Beef Skewers

Ingredients:

For the Marinade:

- 1.5 lbs beef sirloin or flank steak, thinly sliced
- 1/4 cup soy sauce
- 2 tablespoons fish sauce
- 2 tablespoons oyster sauce
- 2 tablespoons brown sugar
- 1 tablespoon sesame oil
- 3 cloves garlic, minced
- 1 tablespoon fresh ginger, grated
- 1 teaspoon chili paste (adjust to taste)
- 1 cup fresh Thai basil leaves, loosely packed
- Wooden skewers, soaked in water for 30 minutes

Additional Skewer Ingredients:

- Cherry tomatoes
- Red bell pepper, cut into chunks
- Red onion, cut into chunks
- Lime wedges (for serving)

Instructions:

For the Marinade:

In a bowl, whisk together soy sauce, fish sauce, oyster sauce, brown sugar, sesame oil, minced garlic, grated ginger, chili paste, and Thai basil leaves to create the aromatic Thai basil beef marinade.
Add the thinly sliced beef to the marinade, ensuring all slices are well-coated. Marinate in the refrigerator for at least 2 hours to allow the flavors to meld.

For Assembling the Skewers:

Preheat your grill to medium-high heat.

Thread the marinated beef slices, cherry tomatoes, red bell pepper chunks, and red onion chunks onto the soaked wooden skewers, alternating between the ingredients.

Grill the skewers for approximately 2-3 minutes per side, or until the beef is cooked to your liking and has a delightful aroma.

Once done, remove the skewers from the grill and let them rest for a few minutes.

Serve the Thai Basil Beef Skewers with lime wedges on the side.

Optionally, serve over jasmine rice or with a side of Thai peanut sauce.

Enjoy these Thai Basil Beef Skewers for a burst of bold and aromatic flavors inspired by Thai cuisine!

Chimichurri Marinated Beef Skewers

Ingredients:

For the Chimichurri Marinade:

- 1.5 lbs beef sirloin or ribeye, cut into cubes
- 1 cup fresh parsley, chopped
- 1/4 cup fresh cilantro, chopped
- 4 cloves garlic, minced
- 1/2 cup red wine vinegar
- 1/2 cup extra-virgin olive oil
- 1 teaspoon dried oregano
- 1 teaspoon red pepper flakes (adjust to taste)
- Salt and black pepper to taste
- Wooden skewers, soaked in water for 30 minutes

Additional Skewer Ingredients:

- Red and yellow bell peppers, cut into chunks
- Red onion, cut into chunks
- Cherry tomatoes

Instructions:

For the Chimichurri Marinade:

In a blender or food processor, combine fresh parsley, fresh cilantro, minced garlic, red wine vinegar, extra-virgin olive oil, dried oregano, red pepper flakes, salt, and black pepper. Blend until you achieve a smooth chimichurri sauce.
Place the beef cubes in a bowl and pour half of the chimichurri sauce over the beef, reserving the other half for basting and serving. Toss the beef in the marinade, ensuring all pieces are well-coated. Marinate in the refrigerator for at least 2 hours.

For Assembling the Skewers:

Preheat your grill to medium-high heat.

Thread the marinated beef cubes, bell pepper chunks, red onion chunks, and cherry tomatoes onto the soaked wooden skewers, alternating between the ingredients.

Grill the skewers for about 8-10 minutes, turning occasionally, until the beef is cooked to your liking and has a nice char.

During grilling, baste the skewers with the reserved chimichurri sauce for added flavor.

Once done, remove the skewers from the grill and let them rest for a few minutes. Serve the Chimichurri Marinated Beef Skewers with an extra drizzle of chimichurri sauce.

Enjoy these zesty and herb-infused Chimichurri Marinated Beef Skewers for a taste of Argentinean cuisine!

Sesame Ginger Beef Skewers

Ingredients:

For the Marinade:

- 1.5 lbs beef sirloin or flank steak, thinly sliced
- 1/4 cup soy sauce
- 2 tablespoons sesame oil
- 2 tablespoons rice vinegar
- 2 tablespoons honey
- 1 tablespoon fresh ginger, grated
- 2 cloves garlic, minced
- 1 tablespoon sesame seeds
- Green onions, thinly sliced (for garnish)
- Wooden skewers, soaked in water for 30 minutes

Additional Skewer Ingredients:

- Red and yellow bell peppers, cut into chunks
- Pineapple chunks

Instructions:

For the Marinade:

In a bowl, whisk together soy sauce, sesame oil, rice vinegar, honey, grated ginger, minced garlic, and sesame seeds to create the sesame ginger marinade.
Add the thinly sliced beef to the marinade, ensuring all slices are well-coated.
Marinate in the refrigerator for at least 2 hours.

For Assembling the Skewers:

Preheat your grill to medium-high heat.
Thread the marinated beef slices, bell pepper chunks, pineapple chunks, and any additional vegetables onto the soaked wooden skewers, alternating between the ingredients.
Grill the skewers for approximately 2-3 minutes per side, or until the beef is cooked to your liking and has a nice sear.
Once done, remove the skewers from the grill and let them rest for a few minutes.
Garnish the Sesame Ginger Beef Skewers with thinly sliced green onions.

Serve over steamed rice or with a side of stir-fried vegetables.

Enjoy these Sesame Ginger Beef Skewers for a delicious blend of sweet, savory, and nutty flavors!

Honey Soy Glazed Beef Skewers

Ingredients:

For the Marinade:

- 1.5 lbs beef sirloin or ribeye, cut into cubes
- 1/4 cup soy sauce
- 2 tablespoons honey
- 2 tablespoons rice vinegar
- 1 tablespoon sesame oil
- 2 cloves garlic, minced
- 1 teaspoon fresh ginger, grated
- 1 tablespoon olive oil
- Wooden skewers, soaked in water for 30 minutes

Additional Skewer Ingredients:

- Red and green bell peppers, cut into chunks
- Red onion, cut into chunks
- Pineapple chunks

Instructions:

For the Marinade:

In a bowl, whisk together soy sauce, honey, rice vinegar, sesame oil, minced garlic, grated ginger, and olive oil to create the honey soy glaze marinade. Place the beef cubes in a resealable plastic bag or shallow dish. Pour the honey soy glaze marinade over the beef, ensuring all pieces are well-coated. Seal the bag or cover the dish and refrigerate for at least 2 hours.

For Assembling the Skewers:

Preheat your grill to medium-high heat.
Thread the marinated beef cubes, bell pepper chunks, red onion chunks, and pineapple chunks onto the soaked wooden skewers, alternating between the ingredients.
Grill the skewers for about 8-10 minutes, turning occasionally, until the beef is cooked to your liking and has a nice caramelized glaze.

Once done, remove the skewers from the grill and let them rest for a few minutes. Optionally, brush some extra honey soy glaze onto the skewers for added sweetness and shine.

Serve the Honey Soy Glazed Beef Skewers over a bed of rice or with a side of steamed vegetables.

Enjoy these delectable Honey Soy Glazed Beef Skewers for a perfect blend of sweet and savory flavors!

Blue Cheese-Stuffed Bacon Wrapped Beef Skew

Ingredients:

For the Blue Cheese Filling:

- 4 oz blue cheese, crumbled
- 2 tablespoons cream cheese
- 2 tablespoons chopped chives

For the Beef Skewers:

- 1.5 lbs beef sirloin or ribeye, cut into cubes
- Salt and black pepper to taste
- 8 slices of bacon, cut in half
- Wooden skewers, soaked in water for 30 minutes

Instructions:

For the Blue Cheese Filling:

In a bowl, mix together crumbled blue cheese, cream cheese, and chopped chives until well combined. Set aside.

For Assembling the Skewers:

Preheat your grill to medium-high heat.
Season the beef cubes with salt and black pepper.
Take a cube of beef and make a small indentation in the center using your thumb.
Spoon a small amount of the blue cheese filling into the indentation.
Wrap each beef cube with half a slice of bacon, securing the bacon with the wooden skewer.
Thread the bacon-wrapped beef skewers onto the soaked wooden skewers, ensuring the bacon is tightly wrapped.
Grill the skewers for about 8-10 minutes, turning occasionally, until the bacon is crispy and the beef is cooked to your liking.
Once done, remove the skewers from the grill and let them rest for a few minutes.
Serve the Blue Cheese-Stuffed Bacon-Wrapped Beef Skewers as a flavorful appetizer or main course.

Enjoy these indulgent and savory skewers with the perfect combination of blue cheese, bacon, and beef!

Seafood Skewers:
Lemon Herb Shrimp Skewers

Ingredients:

For the Marinade:

- 1 lb large shrimp, peeled and deveined
- 3 tablespoons olive oil
- 3 tablespoons fresh lemon juice
- 2 cloves garlic, minced
- 1 teaspoon lemon zest
- 1 tablespoon fresh parsley, chopped
- 1 teaspoon dried oregano
- Salt and black pepper to taste
- Wooden skewers, soaked in water for 30 minutes

Additional Skewer Ingredients:

- Cherry tomatoes
- Yellow bell pepper, cut into chunks
- Red onion, cut into chunks

Instructions:

For the Marinade:

In a bowl, whisk together olive oil, fresh lemon juice, minced garlic, lemon zest, chopped parsley, dried oregano, salt, and black pepper to create the lemon herb marinade.

Place the peeled and deveined shrimp in a bowl and toss them in the marinade, ensuring each shrimp is well-coated. Let it marinate in the refrigerator for about 20-30 minutes.

For Assembling the Skewers:

Preheat your grill to medium-high heat.

Thread the marinated shrimp, cherry tomatoes, yellow bell pepper chunks, and red onion chunks onto the soaked wooden skewers, alternating between the ingredients.

Grill the skewers for approximately 2-3 minutes per side, or until the shrimp are opaque and cooked through.
Once done, remove the skewers from the grill and let them rest for a few minutes.
Serve the Lemon Herb Shrimp Skewers with additional lemon wedges for squeezing.
Optionally, garnish with extra chopped parsley for a burst of freshness.

Enjoy these light and flavorful Lemon Herb Shrimp Skewers as a delightful seafood dish!

Cajun Spiced Salmon Skewers

Ingredients:

For the Cajun Spice Mix:

- 1 tablespoon smoked paprika
- 1 teaspoon onion powder
- 1 teaspoon garlic powder
- 1 teaspoon dried thyme
- 1 teaspoon dried oregano
- 1/2 teaspoon cayenne pepper (adjust to taste)
- Salt and black pepper to taste

For the Salmon Skewers:

- 1 lb salmon fillets, skinless, cut into cubes
- 2 tablespoons olive oil
- 1 tablespoon lemon juice
- Wooden skewers, soaked in water for 30 minutes

Additional Skewer Ingredients:

- Cherry tomatoes
- Red and yellow bell peppers, cut into chunks
- Red onion, cut into chunks
- Lemon wedges (for serving)

Instructions:

For the Cajun Spice Mix:

In a bowl, mix together smoked paprika, onion powder, garlic powder, dried thyme, dried oregano, cayenne pepper, salt, and black pepper to create the Cajun spice mix.

For the Salmon Skewers:

In a separate bowl, combine olive oil and lemon juice. Brush this mixture over the salmon cubes.
Sprinkle the Cajun spice mix over the salmon cubes, ensuring they are well-coated. Marinate for about 15-20 minutes.

For Assembling the Skewers:

- Preheat your grill to medium-high heat.
- Thread the Cajun-spiced salmon cubes, cherry tomatoes, bell pepper chunks, and red onion chunks onto the soaked wooden skewers, alternating between the ingredients.
- Grill the skewers for approximately 3-4 minutes per side, or until the salmon is cooked through and has a nice char.
- Once done, remove the skewers from the grill and let them rest for a few minutes.
- Serve the Cajun Spiced Salmon Skewers with lemon wedges on the side.

Enjoy these Cajun-spiced salmon skewers for a zesty and flavorful seafood experience!

Coconut Lime Grilled Scallop Skewers

Ingredients:

For the Coconut Lime Marinade:

- 1 lb large scallops, cleaned
- 1/2 cup coconut milk
- Zest and juice of 2 limes
- 2 tablespoons soy sauce
- 1 tablespoon honey
- 2 cloves garlic, minced
- 1 teaspoon grated fresh ginger
- 1 tablespoon chopped cilantro
- Salt and black pepper to taste
- Wooden skewers, soaked in water for 30 minutes

Additional Skewer Ingredients:

- Pineapple chunks
- Red and green bell peppers, cut into chunks
- Red onion, cut into chunks

Instructions:

For the Coconut Lime Marinade:

In a bowl, whisk together coconut milk, lime zest, lime juice, soy sauce, honey, minced garlic, grated ginger, chopped cilantro, salt, and black pepper to create the Coconut Lime marinade.

Place the cleaned scallops in a bowl and pour half of the marinade over them. Toss to coat evenly and let them marinate for about 15-20 minutes.

For Assembling the Skewers:

Preheat your grill to medium-high heat.

Thread the marinated scallops, pineapple chunks, bell pepper chunks, and red onion chunks onto the soaked wooden skewers, alternating between the ingredients.

Grill the skewers for approximately 2-3 minutes per side, or until the scallops are opaque and have a nice sear.
During grilling, brush the skewers with the remaining Coconut Lime marinade for added flavor.
Once done, remove the skewers from the grill and let them rest for a few minutes.
Serve the Coconut Lime Grilled Scallop Skewers with a sprinkle of fresh cilantro.

Enjoy these tropical-inspired Coconut Lime Grilled Scallop Skewers for a delightful seafood experience!

Teriyaki Glazed Tuna Skewers

Ingredients:

For the Teriyaki Marinade:

- 1 lb fresh tuna steaks, cut into cubes
- 1/4 cup soy sauce
- 2 tablespoons mirin
- 2 tablespoons sake (optional)
- 2 tablespoons brown sugar
- 1 tablespoon honey
- 1 tablespoon sesame oil
- 2 cloves garlic, minced
- 1 teaspoon fresh ginger, grated
- Wooden skewers, soaked in water for 30 minutes

Additional Skewer Ingredients:

- Pineapple chunks
- Red and green bell peppers, cut into chunks
- Green onions, sliced (for garnish)
- Sesame seeds (for garnish)

Instructions:

For the Teriyaki Marinade:

In a bowl, whisk together soy sauce, mirin, sake, brown sugar, honey, sesame oil, minced garlic, and grated ginger to create the teriyaki marinade.
Place the tuna cubes in a bowl and pour the teriyaki marinade over them, ensuring each piece is well-coated. Marinate in the refrigerator for at least 30 minutes.

For Assembling the Skewers:

Preheat your grill to medium-high heat.
Thread the marinated tuna cubes, pineapple chunks, bell pepper chunks, and green onion slices onto the soaked wooden skewers, alternating between the ingredients.

Grill the skewers for approximately 2-3 minutes per side, or until the tuna is seared on the outside but still pink in the center.
Once done, remove the skewers from the grill and let them rest for a few minutes.
Garnish the Teriyaki Glazed Tuna Skewers with sesame seeds and additional sliced green onions.
Serve over a bed of steamed rice or with a side of stir-fried vegetables.

Enjoy these Teriyaki Glazed Tuna Skewers for a taste of Japanese-inspired grilled goodness!

Mediterranean Grilled Swordfish Skewers

Ingredients:

For the Swordfish Marinade:

- 1.5 lbs swordfish, cut into cubes
- 1/4 cup olive oil
- 2 tablespoons lemon juice
- 3 cloves garlic, minced
- 1 teaspoon dried oregano
- 1 teaspoon dried thyme
- 1 teaspoon smoked paprika
- Salt and black pepper to taste
- Wooden skewers, soaked in water for 30 minutes

Additional Skewer Ingredients:

- Cherry tomatoes
- Red onion, cut into chunks
- Kalamata olives
- Lemon wedges (for serving)

Instructions:

For the Swordfish Marinade:

In a bowl, whisk together olive oil, lemon juice, minced garlic, dried oregano, dried thyme, smoked paprika, salt, and black pepper to create the Mediterranean marinade.
Place the swordfish cubes in a bowl and pour the marinade over them, ensuring each piece is well-coated. Marinate in the refrigerator for at least 30 minutes.

For Assembling the Skewers:

Preheat your grill to medium-high heat.
Thread the marinated swordfish cubes, cherry tomatoes, red onion chunks, and Kalamata olives onto the soaked wooden skewers, alternating between the ingredients.

Grill the skewers for approximately 2-3 minutes per side, or until the swordfish is cooked through and has a nice grill marks.

Once done, remove the skewers from the grill and let them rest for a few minutes.

Serve the Mediterranean Grilled Swordfish Skewers with lemon wedges on the side.

Optionally, drizzle with extra olive oil and sprinkle with additional dried herbs for added flavor.

Enjoy these flavorful and light Mediterranean Grilled Swordfish Skewers as a delicious seafood dish!

Garlic Butter Lobster Skewers

Ingredients:

For the Garlic Butter Marinade:

- 2 lobster tails, shells removed and cut into chunks
- 1/2 cup unsalted butter, melted
- 4 cloves garlic, minced
- 2 tablespoons fresh parsley, chopped
- 1 tablespoon lemon juice
- Salt and black pepper to taste
- Wooden skewers, soaked in water for 30 minutes

Additional Skewer Ingredients:

- Cherry tomatoes
- Lemon wedges (for serving)

Instructions:

For the Garlic Butter Marinade:

In a bowl, combine melted butter, minced garlic, chopped fresh parsley, lemon juice, salt, and black pepper to create the garlic butter marinade.

Place the lobster chunks in a bowl and toss them in the garlic butter marinade, ensuring each piece is well-coated. Marinate in the refrigerator for about 15-20 minutes.

For Assembling the Skewers:

Preheat your grill to medium-high heat.
Thread the marinated lobster chunks and cherry tomatoes onto the soaked wooden skewers, alternating between the ingredients.
Grill the skewers for approximately 2-3 minutes per side, or until the lobster is opaque and cooked through.
Once done, remove the skewers from the grill and let them rest for a few minutes.
Serve the Garlic Butter Lobster Skewers with lemon wedges on the side.
Optionally, brush some extra garlic butter onto the skewers for additional flavor.

Enjoy these indulgent Garlic Butter Lobster Skewers for a rich and savory seafood treat!

Pineapple Glazed Mahi-Mahi Skewers

Ingredients:

For the Pineapple Glaze:

- 1/2 cup pineapple juice
- 1/4 cup soy sauce
- 3 tablespoons honey
- 2 tablespoons rice vinegar
- 1 tablespoon ginger, grated
- 2 cloves garlic, minced
- 1 teaspoon cornstarch (optional, for thickening)
- Salt and black pepper to taste

For the Mahi-Mahi Skewers:

- 1.5 lbs mahi-mahi fillets, cut into cubes
- 1 tablespoon olive oil
- Salt and black pepper to taste
- Wooden skewers, soaked in water for 30 minutes

Additional Skewer Ingredients:

- Pineapple chunks
- Red and green bell peppers, cut into chunks
- Red onion, cut into chunks
- Sesame seeds (for garnish)
- Green onions, sliced (for garnish)

Instructions:

For the Pineapple Glaze:

> In a saucepan, combine pineapple juice, soy sauce, honey, rice vinegar, grated ginger, minced garlic, salt, and black pepper. Bring to a simmer over medium heat.
> If desired, mix cornstarch with a little water to create a slurry and add it to the glaze to thicken. Simmer for an additional 1-2 minutes until the glaze has a syrupy consistency.
> Remove the glaze from heat and set aside.

For the Mahi-Mahi Skewers:

Preheat your grill to medium-high heat.
In a bowl, toss mahi-mahi cubes with olive oil, salt, and black pepper.
Thread the mahi-mahi cubes, pineapple chunks, bell pepper chunks, and red onion chunks onto the soaked wooden skewers, alternating between the ingredients.
Grill the skewers for approximately 3-4 minutes per side, or until the mahi-mahi is cooked through and has grill marks.
During the last minute of grilling, brush the Pineapple Glaze onto the skewers, coating them evenly.
Once done, remove the skewers from the grill and let them rest for a few minutes.
Garnish the Pineapple Glazed Mahi-Mahi Skewers with sesame seeds and sliced green onions.

Serve these delectable Pineapple Glazed Mahi-Mahi Skewers over rice or with a side of your favorite grilled vegetables. Enjoy the tropical flavors!

Cilantro Lime Grilled Snapper Skewers

Ingredients:

For the Cilantro Lime Marinade:

- 1.5 lbs snapper fillets, cut into cubes
- 1/4 cup olive oil
- 1/4 cup fresh cilantro, chopped
- 3 tablespoons lime juice
- 2 cloves garlic, minced
- 1 teaspoon cumin
- 1 teaspoon paprika
- Salt and black pepper to taste
- Wooden skewers, soaked in water for 30 minutes

Additional Skewer Ingredients:

- Cherry tomatoes
- Red and yellow bell peppers, cut into chunks
- Red onion, cut into chunks
- Lime wedges (for serving)
- Fresh cilantro, for garnish

Instructions:

For the Cilantro Lime Marinade:

In a bowl, whisk together olive oil, chopped cilantro, lime juice, minced garlic, cumin, paprika, salt, and black pepper to create the cilantro lime marinade. Place the snapper cubes in a bowl and toss them in the marinade, ensuring each piece is well-coated. Marinate in the refrigerator for at least 30 minutes.

For Assembling the Skewers:

Preheat your grill to medium-high heat.
Thread the marinated snapper cubes, cherry tomatoes, bell pepper chunks, and red onion chunks onto the soaked wooden skewers, alternating between the ingredients.
Grill the skewers for approximately 2-3 minutes per side, or until the snapper is cooked through and has a nice char.

Once done, remove the skewers from the grill and let them rest for a few minutes. Serve the Cilantro Lime Grilled Snapper Skewers with lime wedges on the side. Garnish with fresh cilantro for a burst of color and flavor.

Enjoy these vibrant and zesty Cilantro Lime Grilled Snapper Skewers as a delightful seafood dish!

Spicy Mango Salsa Shrimp Skewers

Ingredients:

For the Spicy Mango Salsa:

- 1 large ripe mango, diced
- 1/4 cup red onion, finely chopped
- 1/4 cup fresh cilantro, chopped
- 1 jalapeño, seeded and finely chopped
- 2 tablespoons lime juice
- Salt and black pepper to taste

For the Shrimp Skewers:

- 1 lb large shrimp, peeled and deveined
- 2 tablespoons olive oil
- 1 teaspoon smoked paprika
- 1 teaspoon ground cumin
- 1/2 teaspoon cayenne pepper (adjust to taste)
- Salt and black pepper to taste
- Wooden skewers, soaked in water for 30 minutes

Additional Skewer Ingredients:

- Red and yellow bell peppers, cut into chunks
- Red onion, cut into chunks
- Lime wedges (for serving)

Instructions:

For the Spicy Mango Salsa:

In a bowl, combine diced mango, finely chopped red onion, chopped cilantro, finely chopped jalapeño, lime juice, salt, and black pepper. Mix well to create the spicy mango salsa. Refrigerate until ready to use.

For the Shrimp Skewers:

In a bowl, mix together olive oil, smoked paprika, ground cumin, cayenne pepper, salt, and black pepper to create a spice rub.

Toss the peeled and deveined shrimp in the spice rub, ensuring each shrimp is well-coated. Marinate for about 15-20 minutes.

For Assembling the Skewers:

Preheat your grill to medium-high heat.

Thread the marinated shrimp, bell pepper chunks, and red onion chunks onto the soaked wooden skewers, alternating between the ingredients.

Grill the skewers for approximately 2-3 minutes per side, or until the shrimp is opaque and has a nice grill marks.

Once done, remove the skewers from the grill and let them rest for a few minutes.

Serve the Spicy Mango Salsa Shrimp Skewers with lime wedges on the side.

Optionally, top the skewers with a generous spoonful of spicy mango salsa before serving.

Enjoy these Spicy Mango Salsa Shrimp Skewers for a perfect combination of heat, sweetness, and citrusy freshness!

Chipotle Lime Grilled Prawn Skewers

Ingredients:

For the Chipotle Lime Marinade:

- 1 lb large prawns, peeled and deveined
- 3 tablespoons olive oil
- 2 tablespoons chipotle peppers in adobo sauce, minced
- 2 tablespoons fresh cilantro, chopped
- 2 tablespoons lime juice
- 2 cloves garlic, minced
- 1 teaspoon ground cumin
- 1 teaspoon smoked paprika
- Salt and black pepper to taste
- Wooden skewers, soaked in water for 30 minutes

Additional Skewer Ingredients:

- Pineapple chunks
- Red and yellow bell peppers, cut into chunks
- Red onion, cut into chunks
- Lime wedges (for serving)

Instructions:

For the Chipotle Lime Marinade:

In a bowl, whisk together olive oil, minced chipotle peppers, chopped cilantro, lime juice, minced garlic, ground cumin, smoked paprika, salt, and black pepper to create the chipotle lime marinade.
Toss the peeled and deveined prawns in the marinade, ensuring each prawn is well-coated. Marinate in the refrigerator for about 15-20 minutes.

For Assembling the Skewers:

Preheat your grill to medium-high heat.
Thread the marinated prawns, pineapple chunks, bell pepper chunks, and red onion chunks onto the soaked wooden skewers, alternating between the ingredients.

Grill the skewers for approximately 2-3 minutes per side, or until the prawns are opaque and have a nice grill marks.
Once done, remove the skewers from the grill and let them rest for a few minutes.
Serve the Chipotle Lime Grilled Prawn Skewers with lime wedges on the side. Optionally, brush some extra chipotle lime marinade onto the skewers for an added burst of flavor.

Enjoy these Chipotle Lime Grilled Prawn Skewers for a spicy and tangy seafood delight!

Vegetarian Skewers:

Caprese Salad Skewers

Ingredients:

- Fresh mozzarella balls (bocconcini), drained
- Cherry tomatoes
- Fresh basil leaves
- Balsamic glaze or reduced balsamic vinegar
- Wooden skewers, soaked in water for 30 minutes

Instructions:

Begin by assembling the Caprese Salad Skewers. Take a wooden skewer and thread a fresh mozzarella ball, followed by a cherry tomato, and then a fresh basil leaf. Repeat this pattern until the skewer is filled, leaving some space at the top for easy handling.

Continue assembling additional skewers until you have the desired quantity.

Arrange the Caprese Salad Skewers on a serving platter.

Just before serving, drizzle balsamic glaze or reduced balsamic vinegar over the skewers for added flavor.

Serve the Caprese Salad Skewers immediately as a refreshing and delightful appetizer.

These Caprese Salad Skewers offer a bite-sized, elegant presentation of the classic Caprese salad with the perfect combination of mozzarella, tomato, basil, and balsamic glaze. Enjoy!

Balsamic Glazed Veggie Skewers

Ingredients:

For the Balsamic Glaze:

- 1/2 cup balsamic vinegar
- 2 tablespoons olive oil
- 2 tablespoons honey
- 2 cloves garlic, minced
- 1 teaspoon dried oregano
- Salt and black pepper to taste

For the Veggie Skewers:

- Cherry tomatoes
- Zucchini, sliced into rounds
- Yellow bell peppers, cut into chunks
- Red onion, cut into chunks
- Mushrooms, cleaned and halved
- Wooden skewers, soaked in water for 30 minutes

Instructions:

For the Balsamic Glaze:

In a small saucepan over medium heat, combine balsamic vinegar, olive oil, honey, minced garlic, dried oregano, salt, and black pepper.
Bring the mixture to a simmer, then reduce the heat to low. Allow it to simmer for about 10-15 minutes, or until the glaze thickens and coats the back of a spoon. Remove from heat and set aside to cool.

For the Veggie Skewers:

Preheat your grill to medium-high heat.
Thread the cherry tomatoes, zucchini rounds, yellow bell pepper chunks, red onion chunks, and mushroom halves onto the soaked wooden skewers, alternating between the vegetables.
Brush the vegetable skewers with the prepared balsamic glaze, ensuring they are well-coated.

Grill the skewers for approximately 8-10 minutes, turning occasionally, or until the vegetables are tender and have grill marks.
Once done, remove the skewers from the grill and let them rest for a few minutes. Serve the Balsamic Glazed Veggie Skewers with any remaining glaze on the side for dipping.

These Balsamic Glazed Veggie Skewers make for a flavorful and colorful side dish or a vegetarian main course option. Enjoy the delicious combination of balsamic sweetness with perfectly grilled veggies!

Grilled Halloumi and Vegetable Skewers

Ingredients:

For the Marinade:

- 1/4 cup olive oil
- 2 tablespoons lemon juice
- 2 cloves garlic, minced
- 1 teaspoon dried oregano
- Salt and black pepper to taste

For the Skewers:

- Halloumi cheese, cut into cubes
- Cherry tomatoes
- Red and yellow bell peppers, cut into chunks
- Red onion, cut into chunks
- Zucchini, sliced into rounds
- Wooden skewers, soaked in water for 30 minutes

Instructions:

For the Marinade:

In a bowl, whisk together olive oil, lemon juice, minced garlic, dried oregano, salt, and black pepper to create the marinade.

For the Skewers:

Preheat your grill to medium-high heat.
Thread the halloumi cheese cubes, cherry tomatoes, bell pepper chunks, red onion chunks, and zucchini rounds onto the soaked wooden skewers, alternating between the ingredients.
Brush the skewers with the prepared marinade, ensuring they are well-coated.
Grill the skewers for approximately 3-4 minutes per side, or until the halloumi is golden and has grill marks.
Once done, remove the skewers from the grill and let them rest for a few minutes.
Serve the Grilled Halloumi and Vegetable Skewers with a drizzle of extra marinade or a side of tzatziki sauce.

Enjoy these Grilled Halloumi and Vegetable Skewers for a delightful and satisfying vegetarian dish that's perfect for summer grilling!

Teriyaki Tofu Skewers

Ingredients:

For the Teriyaki Marinade:

- 1 block firm tofu, pressed and cut into cubes
- 1/4 cup soy sauce
- 2 tablespoons mirin
- 2 tablespoons sake (optional)
- 2 tablespoons brown sugar
- 1 tablespoon honey
- 1 tablespoon sesame oil
- 2 cloves garlic, minced
- 1 teaspoon fresh ginger, grated
- Wooden skewers, soaked in water for 30 minutes

Additional Skewer Ingredients:

- Red and yellow bell peppers, cut into chunks
- Zucchini, sliced into rounds
- Red onion, cut into chunks
- Pineapple chunks

Instructions:

For the Teriyaki Marinade:

In a bowl, whisk together soy sauce, mirin, sake, brown sugar, honey, sesame oil, minced garlic, and grated ginger to create the teriyaki marinade.
Press the tofu to remove excess water and cut it into cubes.
Place the tofu cubes in a bowl and pour the teriyaki marinade over them, ensuring each piece is well-coated. Marinate in the refrigerator for at least 30 minutes.

For Assembling the Skewers:

Preheat your grill to medium-high heat.
Thread the marinated tofu cubes, bell pepper chunks, zucchini rounds, red onion chunks, and pineapple chunks onto the soaked wooden skewers, alternating between the ingredients.

Grill the skewers for approximately 3-4 minutes per side, or until the tofu is golden and has grill marks.
Once done, remove the skewers from the grill and let them rest for a few minutes.
Optionally, brush some extra teriyaki marinade onto the skewers for added flavor.
Serve the Teriyaki Tofu Skewers over a bed of rice or with a side of stir-fried vegetables.

Enjoy these Teriyaki Tofu Skewers for a delicious and satisfying vegetarian option with a burst of sweet and savory teriyaki flavor!

Greek Salad Skewers with Feta

Ingredients:

- Cherry tomatoes
- Cucumber, cut into chunks
- Kalamata olives, pitted
- Red onion, cut into chunks
- Feta cheese, cut into cubes
- Fresh oregano leaves (optional)
- Wooden skewers, soaked in water for 30 minutes

Instructions:

Begin assembling the Greek Salad Skewers by threading cherry tomatoes, cucumber chunks, Kalamata olives, red onion chunks, and cubes of feta onto the soaked wooden skewers. Alternate the ingredients for a colorful and appetizing presentation.

Repeat the threading process until you have assembled the desired quantity of skewers. Optionally, sprinkle fresh oregano leaves over the skewers for an extra burst of flavor. Arrange the Greek Salad Skewers on a serving platter.

Serve these delightful Greek Salad Skewers as a refreshing and easy-to-eat appetizer at your next gathering.

These Greek Salad Skewers with Feta offer all the delicious flavors of a classic Greek salad in a convenient and fun-to-eat skewer form. Enjoy the combination of crisp vegetables, briny olives, and creamy feta!

Indian Spiced Paneer Skewers

Ingredients:

For the Marinade:

- 1 block of paneer, cut into cubes
- 1/4 cup plain yogurt
- 1 tablespoon ginger-garlic paste
- 1 tablespoon garam masala
- 1 teaspoon ground turmeric
- 1 teaspoon ground cumin
- 1 teaspoon ground coriander
- 1/2 teaspoon red chili powder (adjust to taste)
- 1 tablespoon lemon juice
- Salt to taste
- Wooden skewers, soaked in water for 30 minutes

Additional Skewer Ingredients:

- Red and green bell peppers, cut into chunks
- Red onion, cut into chunks
- Cherry tomatoes

Instructions:

For the Marinade:

> In a bowl, whisk together yogurt, ginger-garlic paste, garam masala, ground turmeric, ground cumin, ground coriander, red chili powder, lemon juice, and salt to create the marinade.
> Cut the paneer into cubes and add them to the marinade, ensuring each piece is well-coated. Allow it to marinate for at least 30 minutes, or refrigerate overnight for a deeper flavor.

For Assembling the Skewers:

> Preheat your grill to medium-high heat.
> Thread the marinated paneer cubes, bell pepper chunks, red onion chunks, and cherry tomatoes onto the soaked wooden skewers, alternating between the ingredients.

Grill the skewers for approximately 3-4 minutes per side, or until the paneer is golden and has grill marks.
Once done, remove the skewers from the grill and let them rest for a few minutes.
Optionally, brush some extra marinade onto the skewers for added flavor.
Serve the Indian Spiced Paneer Skewers with a side of mint chutney or your favorite Indian sauce.

Enjoy these Indian Spiced Paneer Skewers as a flavorful and vegetarian addition to your grill!

Pesto Zucchini and Tomato Skewers

Ingredients:

For the Pesto Marinade:

- 1 cup fresh basil leaves
- 1/2 cup grated Parmesan cheese
- 1/3 cup pine nuts
- 2 cloves garlic, minced
- 1/2 cup extra-virgin olive oil
- Salt and black pepper to taste

For the Skewers:

- Zucchini, sliced into rounds
- Cherry tomatoes
- Wooden skewers, soaked in water for 30 minutes

Instructions:

For the Pesto Marinade:

In a food processor, combine fresh basil leaves, grated Parmesan cheese, pine nuts, and minced garlic.
Pulse the ingredients while gradually pouring in the olive oil until you achieve a smooth pesto consistency.
Season the pesto with salt and black pepper to taste. Adjust the seasoning if necessary.

For Assembling the Skewers:

Preheat your grill to medium-high heat.
Thread zucchini rounds and cherry tomatoes onto the soaked wooden skewers, alternating between the vegetables.
Brush the skewers generously with the prepared pesto marinade, ensuring each piece is well-coated.
Grill the skewers for approximately 2-3 minutes per side, or until the zucchini is tender and has grill marks.
Once done, remove the skewers from the grill and let them rest for a few minutes.
Optionally, drizzle some extra pesto over the skewers before serving.

Serve the Pesto Zucchini and Tomato Skewers as a delicious and vibrant side dish or appetizer.

Enjoy these Pesto Zucchini and Tomato Skewers for a burst of fresh and herby flavors in every bite!

Harissa Roasted Vegetable Skewers

Ingredients:

For the Harissa Marinade:

- 2 tablespoons harissa paste
- 2 tablespoons olive oil
- 1 tablespoon tomato paste
- 1 teaspoon ground cumin
- 1 teaspoon ground coriander
- 1 teaspoon smoked paprika
- 2 cloves garlic, minced
- Salt and black pepper to taste

For the Skewers:

- Bell peppers, cut into chunks (assorted colors)
- Zucchini, sliced into rounds
- Red onion, cut into chunks
- Cherry tomatoes
- Wooden skewers, soaked in water for 30 minutes

Instructions:

For the Harissa Marinade:

In a bowl, whisk together harissa paste, olive oil, tomato paste, ground cumin, ground coriander, smoked paprika, minced garlic, salt, and black pepper to create the harissa marinade.

For Assembling the Skewers:

Preheat your grill to medium-high heat.
Thread bell pepper chunks, zucchini rounds, red onion chunks, and cherry tomatoes onto the soaked wooden skewers, alternating between the vegetables.
Brush the skewers generously with the harissa marinade, ensuring each piece is well-coated.
Grill the skewers for approximately 3-4 minutes per side, or until the vegetables are tender and have grill marks.

Once done, remove the skewers from the grill and let them rest for a few minutes. Optionally, drizzle some extra harissa marinade over the skewers before serving. Serve the Harissa Roasted Vegetable Skewers as a flavorful and spicy side dish or appetizer.

Enjoy these Harissa Roasted Vegetable Skewers for a bold and zesty burst of North African-inspired flavors!

Stuffed Mushroom Skewers

Ingredients:

For the Stuffed Mushrooms:

- Large button mushrooms, stems removed and cleaned
- Olive oil for brushing
- Salt and black pepper to taste

For the Filling:

- 1 cup cream cheese, softened
- 1/2 cup grated Parmesan cheese
- 2 cloves garlic, minced
- 1 tablespoon fresh parsley, chopped
- Salt and black pepper to taste

Additional Skewer Ingredients:

- Cherry tomatoes
- Baby spinach leaves
- Wooden skewers, soaked in water for 30 minutes

Instructions:

For the Stuffed Mushrooms:

Preheat your grill to medium-high heat.
Clean the mushrooms and remove the stems.
Brush the mushroom caps with olive oil and season with salt and black pepper.
Grill the mushrooms for about 2-3 minutes per side, or until they start to soften.
Remove the mushrooms from the grill and let them cool slightly.

For the Filling:

In a bowl, mix together cream cheese, grated Parmesan, minced garlic, chopped parsley, salt, and black pepper to create the filling.

For Assembling the Skewers:

Take a grilled mushroom cap and fill the cavity with the cream cheese mixture.
Thread the stuffed mushrooms onto the soaked wooden skewers, alternating with cherry tomatoes and baby spinach leaves.
Continue assembling the skewers until you have the desired quantity.
Grill the skewers for an additional 2-3 minutes per side, or until the tomatoes blister and the spinach wilts slightly.
Once done, remove the skewers from the grill and let them rest for a few minutes.
Serve the Stuffed Mushroom Skewers as an appetizer or a delightful side dish.

These Stuffed Mushroom Skewers offer a delicious combination of creamy filling, grilled mushrooms, and fresh vegetables. Enjoy this flavorful and savory dish at your next gathering!

Sweet and Spicy Pineapple Jalapeño Skewers

Ingredients:

For the Marinade:

- 1/2 cup pineapple juice
- 1/4 cup soy sauce
- 2 tablespoons honey
- 1 tablespoon olive oil
- 1 tablespoon lime juice
- 1 teaspoon grated ginger
- 2 cloves garlic, minced
- 1-2 jalapeños, thinly sliced (adjust to taste)
- Salt and black pepper to taste

For the Skewers:

- Chicken breast, cut into cubes
- Pineapple chunks
- Red and green bell peppers, cut into chunks
- Red onion, cut into chunks
- Wooden skewers, soaked in water for 30 minutes

Instructions:

For the Marinade:

In a bowl, whisk together pineapple juice, soy sauce, honey, olive oil, lime juice, grated ginger, minced garlic, sliced jalapeños, salt, and black pepper to create the marinade.
Reserve a portion of the marinade for basting during grilling.

For Assembling the Skewers:

Place the chicken cubes in a bowl and coat them with the marinade. Let it marinate in the refrigerator for at least 30 minutes.
Preheat your grill to medium-high heat.

Thread the marinated chicken cubes, pineapple chunks, bell pepper chunks, and red onion chunks onto the soaked wooden skewers, alternating between the ingredients.

Grill the skewers for approximately 3-4 minutes per side, basting with the reserved marinade, or until the chicken is cooked through and has a nice char.

Once done, remove the skewers from the grill and let them rest for a few minutes. Serve the Sweet and Spicy Pineapple Jalapeño Skewers hot, garnished with extra sliced jalapeños if desired.

These skewers offer a perfect balance of sweet and spicy flavors with the tropical touch of pineapple. Enjoy the vibrant and zesty taste of these delicious skewers!